45 Saint Patrick's Day Recipes for Home

By: Kelly Johnson

Table of Contents

- Traditional Irish Stew
- Corned Beef and Cabbage
- Colcannon (Mashed Potatoes with Cabbage)
- Irish Soda Bread
- Shepherd's Pie
- Guinness Beef Stew
- Dublin Coddle
- Boxty (Irish Potato Pancakes)
- Irish Lamb Stew
- Potato Leek Soup
- Reuben Sandwich
- Irish Brown Bread
- Shamrock Shake
- Bangers and Mash
- Celtic Knot Rolls
- Bailey's Irish Cream Cheesecake
- Corned Beef Hash
- Irish Coffee
- Whiskey Glazed Salmon
- Irish Cream Chocolate Mousse
- Black and Tan Brownies
- Smoked Salmon Boxty Rolls
- Irish Oatmeal Cookies
- Potato Farls
- Irish Apple Cake
- Lamb and Guinness Pie
- Dubliner Cheese and Guinness Spread
- Irish Cream Chocolate Truffles
- Irish Cream Coffee
- Colcannon Soup
- Irish Cream Bread Pudding
- Guinness Chocolate Cake
- Irish Flag Salad
- Irish Nachos
- Guinness Ice Cream Float

- Irish Tea Cake
- Whiskey Glazed Carrots
- Dubliner Cheese and Bacon Dip
- Irish Potato Bites
- Irish Stout Ice Cream
- Irish Cheddar and Ale Soup
- Leprechaun Hat S'mores
- Irish Cheddar Soda Bread
- Mint Chocolate Chip Cookies
- Irish Whiskey Chocolate Fondue

Traditional Irish Stew

Ingredients:

- 2 pounds lamb stew meat, cut into chunks
- 3 tablespoons vegetable oil
- 2 tablespoons all-purpose flour
- Salt and black pepper, to taste
- 2 onions, chopped
- 3 cloves garlic, minced
- 4 carrots, sliced
- 4 potatoes, peeled and diced
- 2 cups beef or lamb broth
- 1 cup water
- 2 tablespoons tomato paste
- 2 teaspoons Worcestershire sauce
- 2 bay leaves
- 1 teaspoon dried thyme
- Chopped fresh parsley, for garnish

Instructions:

In a large bowl, toss the lamb stew meat with flour, salt, and black pepper until well coated.
In a large Dutch oven or heavy pot, heat vegetable oil over medium-high heat.
Add the floured lamb chunks in batches and brown them on all sides. Remove each batch and set aside.
In the same pot, add chopped onions and minced garlic. Sauté until the onions are softened.
Deglaze the pot by adding a bit of broth and scraping up any browned bits from the bottom.
Return the browned lamb to the pot and add sliced carrots, diced potatoes, beef or lamb broth, water, tomato paste, Worcestershire sauce, bay leaves, and dried thyme. Stir to combine.
Bring the stew to a simmer, then reduce the heat to low. Cover the pot and let it simmer for about 1.5 to 2 hours, or until the lamb is tender.
Check the seasoning and adjust with salt and black pepper if needed.
Once cooked, discard the bay leaves.

Serve the Traditional Irish Stew hot, garnished with chopped fresh parsley. Enjoy the hearty and comforting flavors of this classic Irish stew!

This Traditional Irish Stew is a hearty and comforting dish that features tender lamb, root vegetables, and aromatic herbs. The slow simmering allows the flavors to meld, creating a savory and satisfying meal. Serve it with a slice of Irish soda bread for an authentic experience, and enjoy this classic recipe that's perfect for warming up on chilly days.

Corned Beef and Cabbage

Ingredients:

- 3-4 pounds corned beef brisket with spice packet
- 10 small red potatoes, quartered
- 5 carrots, peeled and cut into large chunks
- 1 large onion, quartered
- 1 small cabbage, cut into wedges
- 4 cloves garlic, minced
- 4 cups water (or enough to cover the brisket)
- Mustard, for serving

Instructions:

Rinse the corned beef brisket under cold water. Pat it dry with paper towels.
Place the brisket in a large pot or Dutch oven. Add the spice packet that came with the corned beef.
Pour in enough water to cover the brisket.
Bring the water to a boil, then reduce the heat to a simmer. Cover and let it simmer for about 2 hours.
Add the quartered potatoes, chunks of carrots, quartered onion, and minced garlic to the pot. Simmer for an additional 15-20 minutes.
Add the cabbage wedges to the pot and simmer for an additional 15 minutes or until the vegetables are tender.
Once everything is cooked, remove the corned beef from the pot and let it rest for a few minutes before slicing.
Arrange the sliced corned beef on a serving platter, surrounded by the vegetables.
Serve the Corned Beef and Cabbage hot with mustard on the side.
Enjoy this classic Irish dish that's perfect for St. Patrick's Day or any hearty meal!

Corned Beef and Cabbage is a traditional Irish-American dish that is often associated with St. Patrick's Day. The brisket is slowly simmered with flavorful spices, and the addition of potatoes, carrots, onion, and cabbage makes it a complete and hearty meal. Serve it with a dollop of mustard for a delicious and comforting experience.

Colcannon (Mashed Potatoes with Cabbage)

Ingredients:

- 4 large russet potatoes, peeled and cut into chunks
- 1/2 head of green cabbage, finely shredded
- 1 cup milk
- 1/2 cup unsalted butter
- Salt and black pepper, to taste
- 4 green onions, finely chopped (optional, for garnish)

Instructions:

Place the potato chunks in a large pot and cover them with cold water. Add a pinch of salt.
Bring the water to a boil and cook the potatoes until they are fork-tender, about 15-20 minutes.
In a separate pot, cook the shredded cabbage in boiling salted water for about 5-7 minutes or until tender. Drain and set aside.
In a small saucepan, heat the milk and butter over low heat until the butter is melted.
Drain the cooked potatoes and return them to the pot.
Mash the potatoes using a potato masher or a ricer.
Gradually add the warm milk and butter mixture to the mashed potatoes, mixing until smooth and creamy.
Fold in the cooked shredded cabbage into the mashed potatoes.
Season the colcannon with salt and black pepper to taste. Adjust the seasoning as needed.
Transfer the colcannon to a serving dish.
Optional: Garnish with finely chopped green onions for added flavor and color.
Serve the Colcannon hot as a side dish.
Enjoy this classic Irish comfort food that combines creamy mashed potatoes with tender cabbage for a delicious and satisfying side dish!

Colcannon is a traditional Irish dish that brings together the simplicity of mashed potatoes with the earthy flavor of cabbage. The addition of butter and warm milk makes the potatoes creamy and rich. Colcannon is a perfect side dish for any meal, but it's especially popular during St. Patrick's Day. Enjoy the comforting and hearty flavors of this classic Irish recipe!

Irish Soda Bread

Ingredients:

- 4 cups all-purpose flour
- 1 teaspoon baking soda (bicarbonate of soda)
- 1 teaspoon salt
- 1 and 3/4 cups buttermilk

Instructions:

Preheat your oven to 425°F (220°C). Dust a baking sheet with a bit of flour or line it with parchment paper.

In a large mixing bowl, whisk together the all-purpose flour, baking soda, and salt. Make a well in the center of the flour mixture.

Pour most of the buttermilk into the well. Reserve a little bit to adjust the consistency if needed.

Using a wooden spoon or your hands, gently stir the flour into the buttermilk until a soft and slightly sticky dough forms. Add more buttermilk if necessary.

Turn the dough onto a floured surface and knead it briefly, shaping it into a round loaf.

Place the loaf onto the prepared baking sheet.

Using a sharp knife, make a deep cross (X) on the top of the dough. This helps the bread to bake evenly.

Bake in the preheated oven for 15 minutes.

Reduce the oven temperature to 400°F (200°C) and continue baking for an additional 20-30 minutes, or until the bread is golden brown and sounds hollow when tapped on the bottom.

Cool the Irish Soda Bread on a wire rack before slicing.

Serve the bread with butter, jam, or your favorite spread.

Enjoy this simple and classic Irish Soda Bread as a delicious accompaniment to your meals!

Irish Soda Bread is a traditional and straightforward recipe that requires minimal ingredients and effort. The use of buttermilk and baking soda creates a light and slightly tangy bread. Enjoy it warm out of the oven with a spread of butter or any topping of your choice. This classic Irish bread is perfect for any occasion, whether it's St. Patrick's Day or a cozy family meal.

Shepherd's Pie

Ingredients:

For the Mashed Potatoes:

- 4 large potatoes, peeled and cut into chunks
- 1/2 cup milk
- 4 tablespoons unsalted butter
- Salt and black pepper, to taste

For the Filling:

- 1 tablespoon vegetable oil
- 1 onion, finely chopped
- 2 carrots, diced
- 2 cloves garlic, minced
- 1.5 pounds ground lamb or beef
- 2 tablespoons all-purpose flour
- 1 cup beef or vegetable broth
- 2 teaspoons tomato paste
- 1 teaspoon Worcestershire sauce
- 1 cup frozen peas
- Salt and black pepper, to taste
- 1 tablespoon fresh thyme leaves (optional, for garnish)

Instructions:

For the Mashed Potatoes:

> Place the potato chunks in a pot and cover them with cold water. Add a pinch of salt.
> Bring the water to a boil and cook the potatoes until they are fork-tender, about 15-20 minutes.
> Drain the cooked potatoes and return them to the pot.
> In a small saucepan, heat the milk and butter over low heat until the butter is melted.
> Mash the potatoes using a potato masher or a ricer. Gradually add the warm milk and butter mixture, stirring until smooth.
> Season the mashed potatoes with salt and black pepper to taste. Set aside.

For the Filling:

    Preheat your oven to 400°F (200°C).
    In a large skillet, heat vegetable oil over medium heat.
    Add chopped onions and diced carrots. Sauté until the vegetables are softened.
    Add minced garlic and cook for an additional 1-2 minutes until fragrant.
    Add the ground lamb or beef to the skillet, breaking it up with a spoon. Cook until browned.
    Sprinkle the flour over the meat mixture and stir to combine.
    Pour in the beef or vegetable broth, tomato paste, and Worcestershire sauce. Stir well and bring the mixture to a simmer. Cook for about 5 minutes, allowing the liquid to thicken.
    Stir in the frozen peas and cook for an additional 2 minutes. Season with salt and black pepper to taste.
    Transfer the meat and vegetable mixture to a baking dish.
    Spoon the mashed potatoes over the top, spreading them evenly to cover the filling.
    Use a fork to create a decorative pattern on the surface of the mashed potatoes.
    Place the baking dish in the preheated oven and bake for about 20 minutes or until the top is golden brown.
    Optional: Sprinkle fresh thyme leaves over the Shepherd's Pie for garnish before serving.
    Serve the Shepherd's Pie hot and enjoy this hearty and comforting dish!

Shepherd's Pie is a classic comfort food that combines a savory meat and vegetable filling with a layer of creamy mashed potatoes on top. This dish is perfect for a cozy family dinner or a hearty meal on a cold day. Customize the filling with your favorite herbs and vegetables for a delicious twist on this timeless recipe.

Guinness Beef Stew

Ingredients:

- 2 pounds stewing beef, cut into chunks
- Salt and black pepper, to taste
- 1/4 cup all-purpose flour, for dredging
- 3 tablespoons vegetable oil
- 2 large onions, chopped
- 4 cloves garlic, minced
- 2 tablespoons tomato paste
- 1 (14.9 ounces) can Guinness Draught or Stout
- 2 cups beef broth
- 2 tablespoons Worcestershire sauce
- 2 bay leaves
- 1 teaspoon dried thyme
- 1.5 pounds potatoes, peeled and cut into chunks
- 1 cup carrots, sliced
- Chopped fresh parsley, for garnish

Instructions:

Season the stewing beef with salt and black pepper. Dredge the beef chunks in flour, shaking off any excess.
In a large Dutch oven or heavy pot, heat vegetable oil over medium-high heat. Brown the beef in batches, making sure not to overcrowd the pot. Transfer the browned beef to a plate and set aside.
In the same pot, add chopped onions and sauté until they are softened.
Add minced garlic and cook for an additional 1-2 minutes.
Stir in tomato paste and cook for another 2 minutes.
Pour in the Guinness beer, scraping up any browned bits from the bottom of the pot.
Return the browned beef to the pot.
Add beef broth, Worcestershire sauce, bay leaves, and dried thyme. Stir to combine.
Bring the stew to a simmer, then reduce the heat to low, cover, and let it simmer for about 1.5 to 2 hours or until the beef is tender.
About 30 minutes before the stew is done, add potatoes and carrots.
Once the vegetables are cooked, discard the bay leaves.

Check the seasoning and adjust with salt and black pepper if needed.
Serve the Guinness Beef Stew hot, garnished with chopped fresh parsley.
Enjoy this rich and flavorful stew that combines the robust taste of Guinness beer with tender beef and hearty vegetables!

Guinness Beef Stew is a hearty and flavorful dish that features the deep and rich flavors of Guinness beer. The slow cooking process allows the beef to become tender and absorb the delicious broth. Serve this stew with crusty bread for a complete and satisfying meal, perfect for a cozy night in or any St. Patrick's Day celebration.

Dublin Coddle

Ingredients:

- 1.5 pounds pork sausages
- 1.5 pounds thick-cut bacon, chopped
- 4 large potatoes, peeled and sliced
- 2 large onions, sliced
- 2 cloves garlic, minced
- 2 tablespoons fresh parsley, chopped
- Salt and black pepper, to taste
- 2 cups chicken or vegetable broth
- 1 cup apple cider or beer (optional)

Instructions:

Preheat your oven to 300°F (150°C).
In a large skillet, brown the sausages over medium heat. Once browned, remove them from the skillet and cut them into halves or thirds.
In the same skillet, cook the chopped bacon until it becomes crispy. Remove excess bacon grease, leaving about 1-2 tablespoons in the skillet.
Add sliced onions to the skillet and sauté until they are softened.
Layer half of the sliced potatoes in the bottom of a large ovenproof casserole dish.
Top the potatoes with half of the sausages, half of the bacon, half of the sautéed onions, half of the minced garlic, and half of the chopped parsley.
Season with salt and black pepper.
Repeat the layers with the remaining ingredients.
Pour the chicken or vegetable broth over the layers. Optionally, you can add apple cider or beer for additional flavor.
Cover the casserole dish with a lid or aluminum foil.
Bake in the preheated oven for about 1.5 to 2 hours, or until the potatoes are tender.
Check the seasoning and adjust with salt and black pepper if needed.
Serve the Dublin Coddle hot, garnished with additional fresh parsley.
Enjoy this traditional Irish comfort dish that combines sausages, bacon, and potatoes in a flavorful broth!

Dublin Coddle is a classic Irish dish that brings together sausages, bacon, and potatoes in a comforting and flavorful casserole. This hearty one-pot meal is easy to prepare and perfect for warming up on a cold day. Serve it with a side of crusty bread and enjoy the delicious combination of savory flavors in this traditional Irish comfort food.

Boxty (Irish Potato Pancakes)

Ingredients:

- 2 cups raw potatoes, peeled and grated
- 1 cup cooked mashed potatoes
- 1 cup all-purpose flour
- 1 cup buttermilk
- 1 egg, beaten
- 1 teaspoon baking soda
- Salt and black pepper, to taste
- Butter or oil for cooking

Instructions:

Place the grated raw potatoes in a clean kitchen towel and squeeze out any excess liquid.
In a mixing bowl, combine the grated raw potatoes, mashed potatoes, and flour.
In a separate bowl, mix buttermilk, beaten egg, baking soda, salt, and black pepper.
Gradually add the wet ingredients to the potato and flour mixture, stirring to combine. The batter should have a thick, pancake-like consistency.
Heat a skillet or griddle over medium heat and add a little butter or oil.
Spoon portions of the batter onto the hot skillet, spreading them into pancake shapes.
Cook the Boxty pancakes for about 3-4 minutes on each side, or until golden brown and cooked through.
Repeat the process with the remaining batter.
Keep the Boxty pancakes warm in a low oven while cooking the rest.
Serve the Boxty hot with your favorite toppings, such as sour cream, chives, or smoked salmon.
Enjoy these traditional Irish Potato Pancakes for a delightful and savory treat!

Boxty, also known as Irish Potato Pancakes, is a traditional Irish dish made with a combination of raw and mashed potatoes. These savory pancakes have a hearty texture and are often enjoyed as a side dish or a breakfast item. Serve them with toppings of your choice for a delicious and comforting Irish treat.

Irish Lamb Stew

Ingredients:

- 2 pounds lamb stew meat, cut into chunks
- Salt and black pepper, to taste
- 1/4 cup all-purpose flour, for dredging
- 3 tablespoons vegetable oil
- 2 large onions, chopped
- 4 carrots, sliced
- 4 potatoes, peeled and diced
- 2 cloves garlic, minced
- 4 cups beef or lamb broth
- 1 cup water
- 2 tablespoons tomato paste
- 2 teaspoons Worcestershire sauce
- 2 bay leaves
- 1 teaspoon dried thyme
- Chopped fresh parsley, for garnish

Instructions:

Season the lamb stew meat with salt and black pepper. Dredge the meat in flour, shaking off any excess.
In a large Dutch oven or heavy pot, heat vegetable oil over medium-high heat.
Brown the lamb in batches, making sure not to overcrowd the pot. Transfer the browned lamb to a plate and set aside.
In the same pot, add chopped onions and sauté until they are softened.
Add minced garlic and cook for an additional 1-2 minutes.
Stir in tomato paste and cook for another 2 minutes.
Return the browned lamb to the pot.
Add beef or lamb broth, water, Worcestershire sauce, bay leaves, and dried thyme. Stir to combine.
Bring the stew to a simmer, then reduce the heat to low, cover, and let it simmer for about 1.5 to 2 hours or until the lamb is tender.
About 30 minutes before the stew is done, add sliced carrots and diced potatoes.
Once the vegetables are cooked, discard the bay leaves.
Check the seasoning and adjust with salt and black pepper if needed.
Serve the Irish Lamb Stew hot, garnished with chopped fresh parsley.

Enjoy this rich and hearty stew that combines tender lamb with flavorful broth and vegetables!

Irish Lamb Stew is a comforting and hearty dish that showcases the delicious flavor of lamb. The slow simmering process allows the meat to become tender and infused with the savory broth. Serve this stew with a slice of Irish soda bread for a complete and satisfying meal, perfect for any occasion or a cozy family dinner.

Potato Leek Soup

Ingredients:

- 3 leeks, cleaned and thinly sliced (white and light green parts only)
- 3 tablespoons unsalted butter
- 4 large potatoes, peeled and diced
- 1 onion, chopped
- 2 cloves garlic, minced
- 6 cups vegetable or chicken broth
- Salt and black pepper, to taste
- 1 bay leaf
- 1 cup whole milk or heavy cream (optional)
- Chopped fresh chives, for garnish

Instructions:

In a large pot, melt the butter over medium heat.
Add the sliced leeks, chopped onion, and minced garlic to the pot. Sauté until the vegetables are softened, about 5-7 minutes.
Add the diced potatoes to the pot and continue to cook for an additional 3-5 minutes.
Pour in the vegetable or chicken broth, and add the bay leaf. Season with salt and black pepper to taste.
Bring the soup to a simmer, then reduce the heat to low, cover, and let it cook for about 20-25 minutes or until the potatoes are tender.
Remove the bay leaf from the soup.
Use an immersion blender to puree the soup until smooth. Alternatively, transfer the soup to a blender in batches and blend until smooth.
Optional: Stir in whole milk or heavy cream to add richness to the soup.
Adjust the seasoning if needed.
Serve the Potato Leek Soup hot, garnished with chopped fresh chives.
Enjoy this creamy and flavorful soup as a comforting and satisfying meal!

Potato Leek Soup is a classic and comforting dish that combines the mild sweetness of leeks with the creamy texture of potatoes. This simple and delicious soup is perfect for warming up on a chilly day. Serve it as a starter or a light meal, and enjoy the rich and satisfying flavors of this traditional soup.

Reuben Sandwich

Ingredients:

- 8 slices rye bread
- 1 pound corned beef, thinly sliced
- 1 cup sauerkraut, drained
- 8 slices Swiss cheese
- 1/2 cup Russian dressing or Thousand Island dressing
- Butter, softened
- Pickles, for serving (optional)

Instructions:

Preheat a griddle or skillet over medium heat.
Lay out 8 slices of rye bread.
On 4 slices of bread, layer equal amounts of corned beef, sauerkraut, and Swiss cheese.
Spread Russian dressing or Thousand Island dressing on the remaining 4 slices of bread.
Place the dressed slices, dressing-side down, on top of the layered slices to form sandwiches.
Butter the outer sides of each sandwich.
Place the sandwiches on the preheated griddle or skillet.
Cook for 3-5 minutes on each side, or until the bread is golden brown and the cheese is melted.
Press down on the sandwiches with a spatula to flatten slightly.
Remove the Reuben sandwiches from the griddle or skillet and let them rest for a minute.
Slice the sandwiches diagonally and serve hot.
Optionally, serve with pickles on the side.
Enjoy this classic Reuben Sandwich with its delicious combination of corned beef, sauerkraut, Swiss cheese, and tangy dressing!

The Reuben Sandwich is a classic deli favorite known for its flavorful combination of corned beef, sauerkraut, Swiss cheese, and tangy dressing. Grilled to perfection, this sandwich is a delicious and satisfying meal. Serve it with pickles on the side for a complete and hearty experience.

Irish Brown Bread

Ingredients:

- 2 cups whole wheat flour
- 1 cup all-purpose flour
- 1 teaspoon baking soda (bicarbonate of soda)
- 1/2 teaspoon salt
- 2 tablespoons unsalted butter, softened
- 1 3/4 cups buttermilk

Instructions:

Preheat your oven to 425°F (220°C). Dust a baking sheet with a bit of flour.
In a large mixing bowl, combine the whole wheat flour, all-purpose flour, baking soda, and salt.
Add the softened butter to the dry ingredients and mix it in with your fingers until the mixture resembles coarse crumbs.
Make a well in the center of the flour mixture.
Pour most of the buttermilk into the well. Reserve a little bit to adjust the consistency if needed.
Using a wooden spoon or your hands, gently stir the flour into the buttermilk until a soft and slightly sticky dough forms. Add more buttermilk if necessary.
Turn the dough onto a floured surface and shape it into a round loaf.
Place the loaf onto the prepared baking sheet.
Using a sharp knife, make a deep cross (X) on the top of the dough. This helps the bread to bake evenly.
Bake in the preheated oven for 15 minutes.
Reduce the oven temperature to 400°F (200°C) and continue baking for an additional 20-25 minutes, or until the bread is golden brown and sounds hollow when tapped on the bottom.
Cool the Irish Brown Bread on a wire rack before slicing.
Serve the bread with butter and enjoy the wholesome and nutty flavor of this traditional Irish brown bread.
This Irish Brown Bread is perfect as a side to soups, stews, or enjoyed on its own as a delicious and hearty snack.
Enjoy the rich, nutty flavor and hearty texture of this traditional Irish Brown Bread!

Irish Brown Bread is a hearty and flavorful bread with a dense and nutty texture. Made with a combination of whole wheat and all-purpose flour, it's a staple in Irish cuisine. Enjoy it sliced and spread with butter or as a side to soups and stews. This simple and wholesome bread is a classic accompaniment to many Irish meals.

Shamrock Shake

Ingredients:

- 2 cups vanilla ice cream
- 1 cup milk
- 1/2 teaspoon peppermint extract
- Green food coloring
- Whipped cream, for topping
- Green sprinkles or colored sugar, for garnish (optional)

Instructions:

In a blender, combine the vanilla ice cream, milk, and peppermint extract.
Add a few drops of green food coloring to achieve the desired shade of green.
Blend until smooth.
Taste the shake and adjust the amount of peppermint extract or food coloring if needed.
Pour the Shamrock Shake into glasses.
Top each shake with a dollop of whipped cream.
Optionally, garnish with green sprinkles or colored sugar.
Serve the Shamrock Shake immediately and enjoy the minty, festive flavor!

The Shamrock Shake is a popular and festive drink, especially around St. Patrick's Day.

This mint-flavored shake is known for its vibrant green color and deliciously sweet taste.

Enjoy it as a fun and refreshing treat during the holiday season or whenever you want to add a touch of green to your day!

Bangers and Mash

Ingredients:

For the Bangers (Sausages):

- 8 pork or beef sausages
- 2 tablespoons vegetable oil

For the Mash (Mashed Potatoes):

- 4 large potatoes, peeled and diced
- 1/2 cup milk
- 4 tablespoons unsalted butter
- Salt and black pepper, to taste

For the Onion Gravy:

- 2 large onions, thinly sliced
- 2 tablespoons vegetable oil
- 2 tablespoons all-purpose flour
- 2 cups beef or vegetable broth
- 1 tablespoon Worcestershire sauce
- Salt and black pepper, to taste

Instructions:

Preheat your oven to 400°F (200°C).
Place the sausages in a baking dish, drizzle with vegetable oil, and bake for about 20-25 minutes or until cooked through and browned.
While the sausages are baking, make the mashed potatoes. Boil the diced potatoes until tender. Drain and mash them with milk, butter, salt, and black pepper until smooth and creamy.
For the onion gravy, heat vegetable oil in a pan over medium heat. Add the sliced onions and sauté until they are softened and golden brown.
Sprinkle flour over the onions and stir well to combine.
Gradually pour in the beef or vegetable broth, stirring constantly to avoid lumps.

Add Worcestershire sauce, salt, and black pepper to the gravy. Simmer until the gravy thickens.
Once the sausages are cooked, serve them on a bed of mashed potatoes.
Pour the onion gravy over the bangers and mash.
Garnish with chopped fresh parsley if desired.
Enjoy this classic British dish of Bangers and Mash with savory sausages, creamy mashed potatoes, and rich onion gravy!

Bangers and Mash is a beloved British dish featuring sausages (bangers) served with mashed potatoes and a flavorful onion gravy. It's a hearty and comforting meal that's easy to prepare and enjoyed by many. The combination of juicy sausages, creamy mashed potatoes, and savory onion gravy makes it a satisfying and delicious choice for a meal.

Celtic Knot Rolls

Ingredients:

For the Dough:

- 4 cups all-purpose flour
- 1/4 cup sugar
- 1 teaspoon salt
- 1 packet (2 1/4 teaspoons) active dry yeast
- 1 cup warm milk (110°F/43°C)
- 1/4 cup unsalted butter, melted
- 2 large eggs

For the Egg Wash:

- 1 egg
- 1 tablespoon water

Instructions:

In a small bowl, combine the warm milk and sugar. Stir to dissolve the sugar. Sprinkle the yeast over the milk mixture, give it a gentle stir, and let it sit for about 5-10 minutes or until it becomes frothy.

In a large mixing bowl, combine the flour and salt.

Make a well in the center of the flour mixture and add the activated yeast mixture, melted butter, and eggs.

Mix the ingredients together until a dough forms.

Turn the dough out onto a floured surface and knead for about 8-10 minutes or until the dough becomes smooth and elastic.

Place the dough in a lightly greased bowl, cover it with a clean kitchen towel, and let it rise in a warm place for 1-1.5 hours or until it has doubled in size.

Punch down the risen dough and turn it out onto a floured surface.

Preheat your oven to 375°F (190°C).

Divide the dough into equal portions and roll each portion into a long rope.

Form each rope into a Celtic knot shape by looping it around itself.

Place the shaped knots on a baking sheet lined with parchment paper.

In a small bowl, whisk together the egg and water to create an egg wash.
Brush the egg wash over the tops of the Celtic knot rolls.
Bake in the preheated oven for about 15-20 minutes or until the rolls are golden brown.
Allow the Celtic Knot Rolls to cool on a wire rack before serving.
Enjoy these beautiful and delicious rolls with their intricate Celtic knot shapes!

Celtic Knot Rolls are not only a delicious addition to any meal but also a visually stunning treat with their intricate knot shapes. These rolls are perfect for special occasions, celebrations, or to add a touch of elegance to your dinner table. The combination of a soft and fluffy interior with a golden brown crust makes them a delightful accompaniment to various dishes.

Bailey's Irish Cream Cheesecake

Ingredients:

For the Crust:

- 1 1/2 cups graham cracker crumbs
- 1/4 cup sugar
- 1/2 cup unsalted butter, melted

For the Cheesecake Filling:

- 24 ounces cream cheese, softened
- 1 cup sugar
- 3 large eggs
- 1 cup sour cream
- 1/4 cup all-purpose flour
- 1/2 cup Bailey's Irish Cream liqueur
- 1 teaspoon vanilla extract

For the Bailey's Ganache:

- 1/2 cup semi-sweet chocolate chips
- 1/4 cup heavy cream
- 2 tablespoons Bailey's Irish Cream liqueur

Instructions:

Preheat your oven to 325°F (163°C). Grease a 9-inch springform pan.
In a medium bowl, combine the graham cracker crumbs, sugar, and melted butter for the crust. Press the mixture into the bottom of the prepared springform pan.
In a large mixing bowl, beat the softened cream cheese and sugar until smooth. Add the eggs one at a time, beating well after each addition.
Mix in the sour cream, flour, Bailey's Irish Cream, and vanilla extract until the batter is well combined and creamy.
Pour the cheesecake filling over the crust in the springform pan.
Bake in the preheated oven for about 50-60 minutes or until the center is set and the edges are slightly golden.
Remove the cheesecake from the oven and let it cool in the pan for about 10 minutes.

Run a knife around the edges of the pan to loosen the cheesecake, then release the springform sides.
Allow the cheesecake to cool completely on a wire rack.
In a small saucepan, heat the heavy cream until it just begins to simmer.
Pour the hot cream over the chocolate chips in a heatproof bowl. Let it sit for a minute, then stir until smooth.
Add Bailey's Irish Cream to the chocolate ganache and mix until well combined.
Pour the Bailey's ganache over the cooled cheesecake, spreading it evenly.
Refrigerate the cheesecake for at least 4 hours, or preferably overnight, to allow it to set.
Once set, slice and serve the Bailey's Irish Cream Cheesecake.
Enjoy this rich and indulgent dessert with the delightful flavor of Bailey's Irish Cream!

Bailey's Irish Cream Cheesecake is a decadent and delightful dessert that combines the creamy goodness of cheesecake with the rich and distinct flavor of Bailey's Irish Cream. This indulgent treat is perfect for special occasions or as a sweet ending to a meal. The graham cracker crust, velvety cheesecake filling, and luscious Bailey's ganache create a dessert that's sure to impress and satisfy your sweet cravings.

Corned Beef Hash

Ingredients:

- 2 cups cooked corned beef, diced
- 4 cups potatoes, peeled and diced
- 1 onion, finely chopped
- 2 tablespoons unsalted butter
- 2 tablespoons vegetable oil
- Salt and black pepper, to taste
- 1/2 teaspoon dried thyme (optional)
- Poached or fried eggs, for serving (optional)
- Chopped fresh parsley, for garnish (optional)

Instructions:

In a large pot, boil the diced potatoes until they are fork-tender. Drain and set aside.
In a large skillet, melt the butter and vegetable oil over medium heat.
Add the chopped onion to the skillet and sauté until it becomes translucent.
Add the diced corned beef to the skillet and cook until it starts to brown.
Stir in the boiled diced potatoes, spreading them evenly in the skillet.
Allow the mixture to cook without stirring too much to allow a golden crust to form on the bottom.
Season the hash with salt, black pepper, and dried thyme (if using). Adjust the seasoning to taste.
Flip portions of the hash with a spatula to allow the other side to crisp up as well.
Continue cooking until the hash is golden brown and crispy on the edges.
Optionally, serve the Corned Beef Hash with poached or fried eggs on top.
Garnish with chopped fresh parsley for a burst of color and freshness.
Serve hot and enjoy this classic breakfast or brunch dish!

Corned Beef Hash is a hearty and flavorful dish that makes excellent use of leftover corned beef. This classic breakfast or brunch option combines diced corned beef, potatoes, and onions, all cooked to perfection in a skillet until crispy and golden brown.

Top it with a poached or fried egg for an extra indulgence, and enjoy a comforting and satisfying meal that's perfect for any time of day.

Irish Coffee

Ingredients:

- 1 cup hot brewed coffee
- 1 to 1.5 ounces (30-45 ml) Irish whiskey
- 1 to 2 teaspoons brown sugar (to taste)
- Whipped cream, for topping

Instructions:

Brew a cup of your favorite hot coffee.
In a heat-resistant glass or mug, add the brown sugar.
Pour the hot brewed coffee over the brown sugar and stir until the sugar is dissolved.
Add the Irish whiskey to the coffee and stir well.
Top the Irish Coffee with a generous dollop of whipped cream.
Optionally, drizzle a little extra whiskey over the whipped cream.
Serve the Irish Coffee hot and enjoy the delightful combination of coffee, Irish whiskey, and creamy whipped topping.
Sip and savor this classic Irish beverage!

Irish Coffee is a simple and delicious hot beverage that combines the rich flavors of coffee with the warmth of Irish whiskey and the indulgence of whipped cream. It's a perfect drink for cozy evenings or as a delightful treat to enjoy with friends. Adjust the sweetness and whiskey amount to suit your taste preferences, and relish in the comforting and spirited experience of Irish Coffee.

Whiskey Glazed Salmon

Ingredients:

For the Salmon:

- 4 salmon fillets
- Salt and black pepper, to taste
- 2 tablespoons olive oil

For the Whiskey Glaze:

- 1/2 cup whiskey (Irish whiskey or your preferred type)
- 1/4 cup brown sugar
- 1/4 cup soy sauce
- 2 tablespoons Dijon mustard
- 2 cloves garlic, minced
- 1 teaspoon grated fresh ginger
- 1 tablespoon olive oil
- 1 tablespoon chopped fresh parsley (for garnish)

Instructions:

Preheat the oven to 400°F (200°C).
Season the salmon fillets with salt and black pepper.
In a large oven-safe skillet, heat olive oil over medium-high heat.
Sear the salmon fillets, skin side down, for about 2-3 minutes or until the skin is crispy and golden.
Flip the salmon fillets and sear for an additional 2 minutes.
While the salmon is searing, prepare the whiskey glaze. In a bowl, whisk together whiskey, brown sugar, soy sauce, Dijon mustard, minced garlic, and grated fresh ginger.
Move the skillet with the seared salmon into the preheated oven.
Pour the whiskey glaze over the salmon fillets.
Bake in the oven for about 8-10 minutes or until the salmon is cooked to your desired doneness.

While the salmon is baking, heat olive oil in a small saucepan. Pour in any remaining whiskey glaze and simmer for a few minutes until it thickens.

Once the salmon is done, spoon the thickened whiskey glaze over the fillets.

Garnish with chopped fresh parsley.

Serve the Whiskey Glazed Salmon hot, with your favorite side dishes.

Enjoy this flavorful and sophisticated dish that combines the richness of salmon with the bold flavors of the whiskey glaze!

Irish Cream Chocolate Mousse

Ingredients:

- 6 ounces (170g) semi-sweet chocolate, finely chopped
- 2 tablespoons unsalted butter
- 3 large eggs, separated
- 1/4 cup granulated sugar
- 1/2 cup Irish cream liqueur
- 1 cup heavy cream
- Chocolate shavings or grated chocolate, for garnish (optional)

Instructions:

In a heatproof bowl, combine the finely chopped chocolate and butter. Melt the chocolate using a double boiler or by microwaving in short intervals, stirring until smooth. Allow it to cool slightly.
In a separate bowl, whisk together the egg yolks and granulated sugar until the mixture is pale and slightly thickened.
Gradually whisk the melted chocolate mixture into the egg yolk mixture until well combined.
Stir in the Irish cream liqueur and mix until smooth.
In another clean, dry bowl, whip the egg whites until stiff peaks form.
Gently fold the whipped egg whites into the chocolate mixture in two or three additions, being careful not to deflate the egg whites.
In yet another bowl, whip the heavy cream until soft peaks form.
Fold the whipped cream into the chocolate mixture until well combined and smooth.
Divide the Irish Cream Chocolate Mousse into serving glasses or bowls.
Refrigerate the mousse for at least 4 hours, or preferably overnight, to allow it to set.
Before serving, garnish with chocolate shavings or grated chocolate if desired.
Enjoy this indulgent and velvety Irish Cream Chocolate Mousse!

Irish Cream Chocolate Mousse is a luxurious and delightful dessert that combines the richness of chocolate with the smooth and creamy flavor of Irish cream liqueur. It's an elegant treat perfect for special occasions or a sweet ending to a festive meal. The combination of silky chocolate and the subtle kick of Irish cream creates a mousse that is both sophisticated and indulgent.

Black and Tan Brownies

Ingredients:

For the Brownie Layer:

- 1 cup unsalted butter, melted
- 2 cups granulated sugar
- 4 large eggs
- 1 teaspoon vanilla extract
- 1 cup all-purpose flour
- 1/2 cup cocoa powder
- 1/4 teaspoon salt

For the Tan Layer:

- 1 cup granulated sugar
- 1/2 cup unsalted butter, softened
- 2 large eggs
- 1 teaspoon vanilla extract
- 1 1/2 cups all-purpose flour
- 1/4 teaspoon baking powder
- 1/4 teaspoon salt

For the Black Layer:

- 1 cup semi-sweet chocolate chips or chunks
- 1/2 cup unsalted butter
- 3/4 cup granulated sugar
- 2 large eggs
- 1 teaspoon vanilla extract
- 3/4 cup all-purpose flour
- 1/4 teaspoon baking powder
- 1/4 teaspoon salt

Instructions:

Preheat your oven to 350°F (175°C). Grease and line a 9x13-inch baking pan with parchment paper, leaving some overhang for easy removal.

For the Brownie Layer: In a large bowl, whisk together the melted butter and granulated sugar. Add the eggs and vanilla extract, and whisk until well combined. In a separate bowl, sift together the flour, cocoa powder, and salt. Gradually add the dry ingredients to the wet ingredients, mixing until just combined. Spread the brownie batter evenly in the prepared pan.

For the Tan Layer: In another bowl, cream together the softened butter and granulated sugar until light and fluffy. Add the eggs and vanilla extract, and beat until well combined. In a separate bowl, whisk together the flour, baking powder, and salt. Gradually add the dry ingredients to the wet ingredients, mixing until just combined. Spread the tan batter evenly over the brownie layer.

For the Black Layer: In a heatproof bowl, melt the chocolate chips or chunks and butter together using a double boiler or by microwaving in short intervals. Once melted, whisk in the granulated sugar. Add the eggs and vanilla extract, and whisk until well combined. In a separate bowl, sift together the flour, baking powder, and salt. Gradually add the dry ingredients to the chocolate mixture, mixing until just combined. Spread the black batter evenly over the tan layer.

Bake in the preheated oven for 35-40 minutes or until a toothpick inserted into the center comes out with a few moist crumbs. The baking time may vary, so start checking around 30 minutes.

Allow the Black and Tan Brownies to cool completely in the pan on a wire rack. Once cooled, use the parchment paper overhang to lift the brownies out of the pan. Place them on a cutting board and cut into squares.

Serve and enjoy these delicious layered brownies!

Black and Tan Brownies are a delightful twist on traditional brownies, featuring three layers with different textures and flavors. The brownie layer provides a rich chocolatey base, the tan layer adds a soft and sweet element, and the black layer introduces a decadent chocolate dimension. These layered brownies are visually appealing and perfect for indulging your sweet tooth.

Smoked Salmon Boxty Rolls

Ingredients:

For the Boxty Pancakes:

- 1 cup raw potatoes, peeled and grated
- 1 cup cooked mashed potatoes
- 1 cup all-purpose flour
- 1 cup buttermilk
- 1 large egg
- 1/2 teaspoon baking soda
- Salt and black pepper, to taste
- Butter or oil for cooking

For the Filling:

- 8 ounces (225g) smoked salmon
- 1/2 cup cream cheese, softened
- 1 tablespoon fresh dill, chopped
- Zest of 1 lemon
- Salt and black pepper, to taste
- Capers for garnish (optional)

Instructions:

For the Boxty Pancakes: In a large bowl, mix together the grated raw potatoes, mashed potatoes, flour, buttermilk, egg, baking soda, salt, and black pepper. Let the batter rest for about 10-15 minutes.
Heat a skillet or griddle over medium-high heat and add a little butter or oil.
Scoop about 1/4 cup of the boxty batter onto the hot skillet, spreading it out into a thin circle. Cook for 2-3 minutes on each side or until golden brown. Repeat with the remaining batter, adding more butter or oil as needed.
For the Filling: In a bowl, mix together the softened cream cheese, chopped dill, lemon zest, salt, and black pepper.
Once the boxty pancakes are cooked, spread a layer of the cream cheese mixture on each pancake.
Place slices of smoked salmon on top of the cream cheese mixture.
Roll up each boxty pancake with the filling, creating a roll.

Optionally, slice the rolls into bite-sized pieces and secure with toothpicks. Garnish with capers if desired.

Serve the Smoked Salmon Boxty Rolls as an appetizer or a light and flavorful snack.

Enjoy these delicious and elegant bites featuring the classic combination of smoked salmon and cream cheese with the added twist of traditional Irish boxty pancakes!

Irish Oatmeal Cookies

Ingredients:

- 1 cup unsalted butter, softened
- 1 cup brown sugar, packed
- 1 cup granulated sugar
- 2 large eggs
- 1 teaspoon vanilla extract
- 2 cups old-fashioned oats
- 2 cups all-purpose flour
- 1 teaspoon baking powder
- 1/2 teaspoon baking soda
- 1/2 teaspoon salt
- 1 cup raisins or currants
- 1 cup chopped nuts (walnuts or pecans), optional

Instructions:

Preheat your oven to 350°F (175°C). Line baking sheets with parchment paper.
In a large mixing bowl, cream together the softened butter, brown sugar, and granulated sugar until light and fluffy.
Add the eggs one at a time, beating well after each addition. Stir in the vanilla extract.
In a separate bowl, combine the old-fashioned oats, all-purpose flour, baking powder, baking soda, and salt.
Gradually add the dry ingredients to the wet ingredients, mixing until just combined.
Fold in the raisins or currants and chopped nuts, if using.
Drop rounded tablespoons of cookie dough onto the prepared baking sheets, leaving enough space between each cookie.
Bake in the preheated oven for 10-12 minutes or until the edges are golden brown.
Allow the cookies to cool on the baking sheets for a few minutes before transferring them to a wire rack to cool completely.
Store the Irish Oatmeal Cookies in an airtight container.
Enjoy these classic oatmeal cookies with a touch of Irish flair!

These Irish Oatmeal Cookies are a delightful treat with a hearty texture and a perfect blend of sweetness. Packed with oats, raisins, and optional nuts, these cookies have a comforting and satisfying flavor. Whether enjoyed with a cup of tea or as a snack on the go, these cookies capture the warmth of traditional Irish baking.

Potato Farls

Ingredients:

- 2 large potatoes, peeled and diced
- Salt, to taste
- 2 tablespoons unsalted butter
- 1 cup all-purpose flour, plus extra for dusting
- Butter or oil, for frying

Instructions:

Place the diced potatoes in a pot of cold, salted water. Bring to a boil and cook until the potatoes are tender.

Drain the cooked potatoes and return them to the pot. Mash them thoroughly, ensuring there are no lumps. Add the butter and continue mashing until the butter is fully incorporated.

Allow the mashed potatoes to cool slightly.

Gradually add the flour to the mashed potatoes, mixing well to form a dough. You may not need the full cup of flour, so add it gradually until the dough comes together and isn't too sticky.

Turn the dough out onto a floured surface. Roll it into a round disc, about 1/2 inch thick.

Cut the disc into quarters to form farls.

Heat a griddle or a large, flat skillet over medium heat. Add a little butter or oil.

Cook the farls on the griddle for about 5-7 minutes on each side or until they are golden brown and cooked through.

Remove the farls from the griddle and cut each quarter into two triangular pieces.

Serve the Potato Farls hot, with butter or your favorite topping.

Enjoy these traditional Irish potato flatbreads as a side dish or for breakfast with eggs and bacon!

Potato Farls are a traditional Irish dish that is quick and easy to make. These potato flatbreads are a delicious addition to an Irish breakfast or a tasty side dish served with butter. The combination of mashed potatoes and flour creates a dough that is griddled to perfection, resulting in golden brown and flavorful farls.

Irish Apple Cake

Ingredients:

For the Cake:

- 2 cups all-purpose flour
- 1 teaspoon baking powder
- 1/4 teaspoon salt
- 1/2 cup unsalted butter, softened
- 1 cup granulated sugar
- 2 large eggs
- 1 teaspoon vanilla extract
- 1/2 cup milk

For the Apple Filling:

- 2 large apples, peeled, cored, and thinly sliced
- 2 tablespoons granulated sugar
- 1 teaspoon ground cinnamon

For the Topping:

- 2 tablespoons unsalted butter, melted
- 2 tablespoons granulated sugar
- 1/2 teaspoon ground cinnamon

Instructions:

Preheat your oven to 350°F (175°C). Grease and flour a 9-inch round cake pan.
In a medium bowl, whisk together the flour, baking powder, and salt.
In a large mixing bowl, cream together the softened butter and sugar until light and fluffy.
Add the eggs one at a time, beating well after each addition. Stir in the vanilla extract.

Gradually add the dry ingredients to the wet ingredients, alternating with the milk. Begin and end with the dry ingredients. Mix until just combined.

In a separate bowl, toss the thinly sliced apples with sugar and cinnamon for the filling.

Spread half of the cake batter into the prepared cake pan.

Arrange the apple slices over the batter.

Spoon the remaining batter over the apples and spread it evenly.

For the topping, mix together melted butter, sugar, and cinnamon. Drizzle the mixture over the top of the batter.

Bake in the preheated oven for 40-50 minutes or until a toothpick inserted into the center comes out clean.

Allow the Irish Apple Cake to cool in the pan for about 10 minutes before transferring it to a wire rack to cool completely.

Slice and serve the cake, either warm or at room temperature.

Enjoy this delicious and moist Irish Apple Cake on its own or with a dollop of whipped cream!

Irish Apple Cake is a delightful dessert that captures the flavors of tender apples and warm spices. This moist and flavorful cake is a perfect treat to enjoy with a cup of tea or coffee. The combination of a soft cake layer with a cinnamon-sugar apple filling makes this traditional Irish dessert a comforting and delicious choice for any occasion.

Lamb and Guinness Pie

Ingredients:

For the Filling:

- 2 tablespoons vegetable oil
- 2 pounds (about 1 kg) lamb stew meat, cut into bite-sized pieces
- Salt and black pepper, to taste
- 1 large onion, chopped
- 2 carrots, peeled and diced
- 3 cloves garlic, minced
- 1/4 cup all-purpose flour
- 1 can (14.9 ounces) Guinness Stout or other stout beer
- 1 cup beef or lamb broth
- 2 tablespoons tomato paste
- 1 tablespoon Worcestershire sauce
- 2 teaspoons dried thyme
- 2 bay leaves

For the Pastry:

- 2 sheets of store-bought puff pastry, thawed
- 1 egg, beaten (for egg wash)

Instructions:

Preheat your oven to 375°F (190°C).
In a large, oven-safe pot or Dutch oven, heat the vegetable oil over medium-high heat.
Season the lamb stew meat with salt and black pepper. Brown the meat in batches, ensuring each piece gets a good sear. Remove the browned meat and set it aside.
In the same pot, add the chopped onion, diced carrots, and minced garlic. Cook until the vegetables are softened.
Sprinkle the flour over the vegetables and stir well to coat.
Pour in the Guinness Stout and scrape the bottom of the pot to deglaze, releasing any flavorful bits.

Add the browned lamb back to the pot, along with beef or lamb broth, tomato paste, Worcestershire sauce, dried thyme, and bay leaves. Stir to combine.
Bring the mixture to a simmer, then cover the pot and transfer it to the preheated oven.
Bake for about 1.5 to 2 hours or until the lamb is tender and the flavors meld together. Check occasionally and add more broth if needed.
Once the lamb filling is ready, remove the bay leaves and discard them.
Increase the oven temperature to 400°F (200°C).
Roll out the thawed puff pastry sheets on a lightly floured surface to fit the top of your pie dish.
Spoon the lamb filling into a pie dish.
Cover the filling with the rolled-out puff pastry, trimming any excess and crimping the edges to seal the pie.
Brush the top of the pastry with beaten egg for a golden finish.
Cut a few slits in the pastry to allow steam to escape.
Place the pie in the oven and bake for 20-25 minutes or until the pastry is golden brown and puffed.
Remove from the oven and let it cool slightly before serving.
Enjoy this hearty and flavorful Lamb and Guinness Pie!

This Lamb and Guinness Pie is a delicious and comforting dish that combines tender lamb stewed in a rich Guinness-based sauce, all encased in a flaky puff pastry crust. It's a perfect choice for a cozy dinner on a cold day, and the deep flavors of the Guinness Stout add a unique depth to the filling. Serve with your favorite sides and savor the warmth and heartiness of this classic Irish pie.

Dubliner Cheese and Guinness Spread

Ingredients:

- 8 ounces (about 2 cups) Dubliner cheese, grated
- 4 ounces cream cheese, softened
- 1/4 cup Guinness Stout (or other stout beer)
- 1 tablespoon whole grain mustard
- 1 clove garlic, minced
- 1/4 teaspoon black pepper
- Chopped fresh chives or green onions, for garnish (optional)
- Crackers or sliced baguette, for serving

Instructions:

In a mixing bowl, combine the grated Dubliner cheese and softened cream cheese.
Pour in the Guinness Stout and mix well until the cheeses are combined and the mixture is smooth.
Add the whole grain mustard, minced garlic, and black pepper. Mix again until all the ingredients are well incorporated.
Taste the spread and adjust the seasoning if needed.
If desired, garnish with chopped fresh chives or green onions for a pop of color and additional flavor.
Transfer the Dubliner Cheese and Guinness Spread to a serving bowl.
Serve the spread with crackers or sliced baguette.
Enjoy this flavorful and creamy cheese spread with the distinct taste of Dubliner cheese and the richness of Guinness Stout!

This Dubliner Cheese and Guinness Spread is a delightful appetizer or snack that brings together the nutty and sharp flavors of Dubliner cheese with the deep and malty notes of Guinness Stout. The addition of cream cheese adds a creamy texture, making it the perfect spread for crackers or slices of baguette. It's a wonderful addition to any party or gathering, showcasing the rich and distinct tastes of Ireland.

Irish Cream Chocolate Truffles

Ingredients:

- 8 ounces (about 1 1/3 cups) semi-sweet or dark chocolate, finely chopped
- 1/2 cup heavy cream
- 2 tablespoons unsalted butter, softened
- 3 tablespoons Irish cream liqueur
- Cocoa powder, powdered sugar, or finely chopped nuts for coating

Instructions:

Place the finely chopped chocolate in a heatproof bowl.
In a small saucepan, heat the heavy cream over medium heat until it just begins to simmer.
Pour the hot cream over the chopped chocolate. Let it sit for a minute to melt the chocolate.
Stir the chocolate and cream mixture until smooth and well combined.
Add the softened butter and Irish cream liqueur to the chocolate mixture. Stir until the butter is fully melted and the mixture is smooth.
Cover the bowl with plastic wrap and refrigerate for at least 2 hours or until the mixture is firm enough to handle.
Once the chocolate mixture has chilled, use a spoon or a melon baller to scoop out small portions.
Roll each portion into a ball and place them on a parchment-lined tray.
If desired, roll the truffles in cocoa powder, powdered sugar, or finely chopped nuts for coating. Place them back on the tray.
Refrigerate the truffles for another 30 minutes to set.
Once set, transfer the Irish Cream Chocolate Truffles to an airtight container and store in the refrigerator until ready to serve.
Enjoy these rich and decadent truffles with the delightful flavor of Irish cream!

These Irish Cream Chocolate Truffles are a luxurious and indulgent treat perfect for special occasions or as a sweet gift. The combination of rich chocolate, velvety cream, and the subtle kick of Irish cream liqueur creates a melt-in-your-mouth experience. Customize them with your favorite coating, and savor the decadence of these homemade truffles.

Irish Cream Coffee

Ingredients:

- 1 cup hot brewed coffee
- 1 to 1.5 ounces (30-45 ml) Irish cream liqueur (such as Baileys)
- Whipped cream, for topping (optional)
- Chocolate shavings or cocoa powder, for garnish (optional)

Instructions:

Brew a cup of your favorite hot coffee.
In a heat-resistant mug, pour the desired amount of Irish cream liqueur.
Pour the hot brewed coffee over the Irish cream, and stir gently to combine.
Optionally, top the Irish Cream Coffee with a dollop of whipped cream.
Garnish with chocolate shavings or a sprinkle of cocoa powder if desired.
Serve immediately and enjoy this delightful and comforting Irish Cream Coffee!

Irish Cream Coffee is a delicious and cozy beverage that combines the rich flavors of coffee with the creamy and smooth taste of Irish cream liqueur. It's a perfect treat to enjoy on a chilly day, after dinner, or as a festive drink during special occasions. Customize it with whipped cream and chocolate garnishes for an extra touch of indulgence.

Colcannon Soup

Ingredients:

- 3 tablespoons unsalted butter
- 1 onion, finely chopped
- 2 leeks, cleaned and thinly sliced
- 2 cloves garlic, minced
- 4 cups potatoes, peeled and diced
- 4 cups cabbage, shredded
- 6 cups chicken or vegetable broth
- Salt and black pepper, to taste
- 1 cup kale, chopped
- 1 cup milk or cream
- Chives, chopped (for garnish)

Instructions:

In a large pot, melt the butter over medium heat.
Add the chopped onion and sliced leeks. Cook until softened, about 5-7 minutes.
Stir in the minced garlic and cook for an additional minute until fragrant.
Add the diced potatoes and shredded cabbage to the pot. Stir to combine with the vegetables.
Pour in the chicken or vegetable broth, and season with salt and black pepper to taste.
Bring the soup to a boil, then reduce the heat to low. Cover and simmer for about 15-20 minutes or until the potatoes are tender.
Add the chopped kale to the soup and cook for an additional 5 minutes until the kale is wilted.
Using an immersion blender, blend the soup until you reach your desired level of creaminess. Alternatively, transfer a portion of the soup to a blender and blend until smooth, then return it to the pot.
Pour in the milk or cream, stirring to combine. Adjust the seasoning if necessary.
Serve the Colcannon Soup hot, garnished with chopped chives.
Enjoy this hearty and flavorful soup that combines the traditional Irish colcannon ingredients in a comforting and satisfying bowl!

Colcannon Soup is a delicious twist on the classic Irish dish, combining the flavors of potatoes, cabbage, and kale in a creamy and comforting soup. This hearty soup is perfect for cold days and brings together the rich and earthy tastes of the traditional colcannon with the warmth of a bowl of soup. Serve it with a side of crusty bread for a complete and satisfying meal.

Irish Cream Bread Pudding

Ingredients:

- 8 cups cubed day-old bread (such as French or challah)
- 1/2 cup raisins or currants
- 4 large eggs
- 1 cup granulated sugar
- 2 cups whole milk
- 1 cup heavy cream
- 1/2 cup Irish cream liqueur (such as Baileys)
- 1 teaspoon vanilla extract
- 1/2 teaspoon ground cinnamon
- 1/4 teaspoon salt
- Whiskey Sauce (see below)
- Whipped cream, for serving (optional)

Instructions:

Preheat your oven to 350°F (175°C). Grease a 9x13-inch baking dish.
In a large bowl, combine the cubed bread and raisins or currants. Spread the mixture evenly in the prepared baking dish.
In another bowl, whisk together the eggs and sugar until well combined.
In a saucepan over medium heat, warm the milk and heavy cream until it just begins to simmer. Remove from heat.
Slowly pour the hot milk mixture into the egg and sugar mixture, whisking constantly to prevent curdling.
Add the Irish cream liqueur, vanilla extract, ground cinnamon, and salt to the mixture. Whisk until everything is well combined.
Pour the custard mixture over the bread cubes, ensuring that all the bread is soaked.
Let the bread pudding sit for about 15-20 minutes, allowing the bread to absorb the custard.
Bake in the preheated oven for 45-55 minutes or until the top is golden brown and the center is set.
While the bread pudding is baking, prepare the Whiskey Sauce (see below).
Remove the bread pudding from the oven and let it cool slightly before serving.

Serve the Irish Cream Bread Pudding warm, drizzled with Whiskey Sauce and topped with whipped cream if desired.

Whiskey Sauce:

Ingredients:

- 1/2 cup unsalted butter
- 1 cup powdered sugar
- 1/4 cup Irish whiskey

Instructions:

In a saucepan over medium heat, melt the butter.
Stir in the powdered sugar until well combined.
Gradually add the Irish whiskey, stirring continuously until the sauce is smooth.
Remove from heat and let it cool slightly before drizzling over the bread pudding.

Enjoy this rich and indulgent Irish Cream Bread Pudding with the flavorful addition of Irish cream liqueur, perfect for a festive dessert or special occasion!

Guinness Chocolate Cake

Ingredients:

For the Cake:

- 1 cup Guinness Stout
- 1 cup unsalted butter, cubed
- 3/4 cup unsweetened cocoa powder
- 2 cups all-purpose flour
- 2 cups granulated sugar
- 1 1/2 teaspoons baking soda
- 3/4 teaspoon salt
- 2 large eggs
- 2/3 cup sour cream

For the Cream Cheese Frosting:

- 8 ounces cream cheese, softened
- 1 1/4 cups powdered sugar
- 1/2 cup heavy cream

Instructions:

Preheat your oven to 350°F (175°C). Grease and flour a 9-inch round cake pan.
In a saucepan, heat the Guinness and cubed butter over medium heat until the butter is melted. Remove from heat.
Whisk in the cocoa powder until smooth. Let the mixture cool slightly.
In a large mixing bowl, whisk together the flour, sugar, baking soda, and salt.
In another bowl, beat the eggs and sour cream until well combined.
Pour the Guinness mixture into the flour mixture and stir until just combined.
Add the egg and sour cream mixture to the batter and mix until smooth.
Pour the batter into the prepared cake pan.
Bake in the preheated oven for 45-50 minutes or until a toothpick inserted into the center comes out clean.
Allow the cake to cool in the pan for about 10 minutes, then transfer it to a wire rack to cool completely.

For the cream cheese frosting, beat the softened cream cheese and powdered sugar until smooth and creamy.

In a separate bowl, whip the heavy cream until stiff peaks form.

Gently fold the whipped cream into the cream cheese mixture until well combined.

Once the cake has cooled, spread the cream cheese frosting over the top.

Optionally, decorate the cake with additional cocoa powder or chocolate shavings.

Slice and enjoy this moist and rich Guinness Chocolate Cake!

This Guinness Chocolate Cake is a moist and decadent treat with a deep chocolate flavor enhanced by the addition of Guinness Stout. Topped with a luscious cream cheese frosting, it's a perfect dessert for St. Patrick's Day or any celebration. The stout adds a unique richness to the cake, making it a delightful and indulgent choice for chocolate lovers.

Irish Flag Salad

Ingredients:

For the Orange Layer:

- 2 large oranges, peeled and segmented

For the White Layer:

- 2 cups jicama, peeled and julienned

For the Green Layer:

- 2 cups baby spinach leaves

For the Dressing:

- 3 tablespoons olive oil
- 2 tablespoons white wine vinegar
- 1 teaspoon Dijon mustard
- Salt and black pepper, to taste

Instructions:

Arrange the orange segments in the bottom third of a serving dish to represent the orange layer of the Irish flag.
In the middle third of the dish, create the white layer by arranging the julienned jicama.
Finally, place the baby spinach leaves in the top third to represent the green layer.
In a small bowl, whisk together the olive oil, white wine vinegar, Dijon mustard, salt, and black pepper to create the dressing.
Drizzle the dressing over the salad just before serving.
Gently toss the salad to combine the layers and evenly coat with the dressing.
Serve the Irish Flag Salad immediately and enjoy a refreshing and colorful representation of the Irish flag in a healthy salad!

This Irish Flag Salad is a vibrant and fresh way to celebrate the colors of Ireland's flag. With layers of orange, white, and green, this salad is not only visually appealing but also delicious and nutritious. The combination of orange segments, jicama, and spinach makes for a refreshing and crisp salad, perfect for a St. Patrick's Day celebration or any occasion where you want to add a touch of Irish flair to your table.

Irish Nachos

Ingredients:

- 1 pound russet potatoes, washed and thinly sliced
- 2 tablespoons olive oil
- 1 teaspoon garlic powder
- 1 teaspoon onion powder
- 1/2 teaspoon paprika
- 1/2 teaspoon dried thyme
- Salt and black pepper, to taste
- 1 cup shredded cheddar cheese
- 1/2 cup cooked and crumbled bacon
- 1/4 cup sliced green onions
- Sour cream, for dipping

Instructions:

Preheat your oven to 400°F (200°C). Line a baking sheet with parchment paper.
In a large bowl, toss the thinly sliced potatoes with olive oil, garlic powder, onion powder, paprika, dried thyme, salt, and black pepper until the potatoes are evenly coated.
Arrange the seasoned potato slices in a single layer on the prepared baking sheet.
Bake in the preheated oven for 20-25 minutes or until the potatoes are golden brown and crispy, flipping them halfway through the cooking time.
Remove the baked potato slices from the oven and sprinkle them with shredded cheddar cheese.
Return the baking sheet to the oven for an additional 3-5 minutes or until the cheese is melted and bubbly.
Remove from the oven and sprinkle the Irish Nachos with crumbled bacon and sliced green onions.
Serve the Irish Nachos hot with a side of sour cream for dipping.
Enjoy these crispy and flavorful Irish Nachos as a delicious appetizer or snack!

These Irish Nachos are a tasty twist on the classic nachos, featuring crispy potato slices as the base instead of traditional tortilla chips. Loaded with melted cheese, crispy bacon, and fresh green onions, they make a delightful appetizer or snack, perfect for St.

Patrick's Day celebrations or any gathering where you want to add a touch of Irish-inspired flavor.

Guinness Ice Cream Float

Ingredients:

- 1 pint (2 cups) vanilla ice cream
- 1 can (14.9 ounces) Guinness Stout (or other stout beer)
- Chocolate syrup, for drizzling (optional)
- Whipped cream, for topping (optional)
- Maraschino cherry, for garnish (optional)

Instructions:

Scoop the vanilla ice cream into a large glass or beer mug.
Slowly pour the Guinness Stout over the ice cream. Be cautious as the beer may foam.
Drizzle chocolate syrup over the top if desired.
Optionally, top the float with a generous dollop of whipped cream.
Garnish with a maraschino cherry if you like.
Serve immediately and enjoy this unique and delicious Guinness Ice Cream Float!

This Guinness Ice Cream Float is a delightful adult twist on the classic ice cream float, combining the rich and malty flavors of Guinness Stout with creamy vanilla ice cream. The result is a creamy and indulgent treat with a unique depth of flavor. Drizzle with chocolate syrup, top with whipped cream, and garnish with a cherry for an extra touch of sweetness. It's a perfect dessert or beverage for St. Patrick's Day or any occasion where you want to savor the richness of Guinness in a fun and refreshing way.

Irish Tea Cake

Ingredients:

- 2 cups all-purpose flour
- 1 1/2 teaspoons baking powder
- 1/2 teaspoon baking soda
- 1/2 teaspoon salt
- 1/2 cup unsalted butter, softened
- 1 cup granulated sugar
- 2 large eggs
- 1 teaspoon vanilla extract
- 1 cup plain yogurt or buttermilk
- Zest of 1 lemon (optional)
- Confectioners' sugar, for dusting

Instructions:

Preheat your oven to 350°F (175°C). Grease and flour a 9-inch round cake pan.
In a medium bowl, whisk together the flour, baking powder, baking soda, and salt. Set aside.
In a large mixing bowl, cream together the softened butter and granulated sugar until light and fluffy.
Add the eggs one at a time, beating well after each addition. Stir in the vanilla extract.
Gradually add the dry ingredients to the wet ingredients, alternating with the yogurt or buttermilk. Begin and end with the dry ingredients. Mix until just combined.
If using, fold in the lemon zest.
Pour the batter into the prepared cake pan and smooth the top with a spatula.
Bake in the preheated oven for 30-35 minutes or until a toothpick inserted into the center comes out clean.
Allow the cake to cool in the pan for about 10 minutes before transferring it to a wire rack to cool completely.
Once the cake is completely cooled, dust the top with confectioners' sugar.
Slice and enjoy this simple and delicious Irish Tea Cake with a cup of your favorite tea!

This Irish Tea Cake is a classic and versatile treat that is perfect for serving during tea time or as a delightful dessert. The moist and tender cake has a lovely crumb and a hint of sweetness, making it a wonderful accompaniment to a hot cup of tea. The addition of lemon zest adds a subtle citrusy flavor that enhances the overall experience. Whether enjoyed on its own or with a dollop of whipped cream, this Irish Tea Cake is sure to be a hit.

Whiskey Glazed Carrots

Ingredients:

- 1 pound baby carrots, or peeled and sliced carrots
- 2 tablespoons unsalted butter
- 2 tablespoons brown sugar
- 1/4 cup Irish whiskey
- Salt and black pepper, to taste
- Fresh parsley, chopped, for garnish (optional)

Instructions:

In a saucepan, bring water to a boil. Add the baby carrots and cook for about 5-7 minutes or until they are just tender. Drain and set aside.
In a large skillet over medium heat, melt the butter.
Add the brown sugar to the melted butter, stirring until the sugar is dissolved.
Add the cooked carrots to the skillet, tossing them to coat with the butter and sugar mixture.
Pour the Irish whiskey over the carrots and continue to cook for 3-5 minutes, allowing the whiskey to reduce and glaze the carrots.
Season with salt and black pepper to taste. Adjust the seasoning if necessary.
Transfer the glazed carrots to a serving dish.
Garnish with chopped fresh parsley if desired.
Serve the Whiskey Glazed Carrots hot as a flavorful and slightly boozy side dish.

Enjoy these Whiskey Glazed Carrots as a delicious side to complement your meals. The sweet and savory glaze, enriched with the depth of Irish whiskey, adds a unique twist to classic cooked carrots. This side dish is perfect for special occasions or any time you want to elevate your carrot game with a touch of whiskey-infused flavor.

Dubliner Cheese and Bacon Dip

Ingredients:

- 8 ounces cream cheese, softened
- 1 cup sour cream
- 1 cup shredded Dubliner cheese (or sharp cheddar)
- 1 cup cooked and crumbled bacon
- 2 green onions, finely chopped
- 1 teaspoon Worcestershire sauce
- 1/2 teaspoon garlic powder
- Salt and black pepper, to taste
- Fresh parsley, chopped, for garnish (optional)

Instructions:

In a mixing bowl, combine the softened cream cheese and sour cream. Mix until smooth and well combined.
Add the shredded Dubliner cheese, crumbled bacon, chopped green onions, Worcestershire sauce, and garlic powder to the bowl. Mix thoroughly.
Season the dip with salt and black pepper to taste. Adjust the seasoning if needed.
Transfer the dip to a serving dish.
Garnish with chopped fresh parsley if desired.
Refrigerate the Dubliner Cheese and Bacon Dip for at least 1 hour before serving to allow the flavors to meld.
Serve the dip with crackers, tortilla chips, or vegetable sticks.
Enjoy this flavorful and indulgent Dubliner Cheese and Bacon Dip as a delicious appetizer or party snack!

This Dubliner Cheese and Bacon Dip is a rich and savory appetizer that combines the nutty and tangy flavors of Dubliner cheese with the smokiness of bacon. It's perfect for entertaining guests or for a cozy night in. Serve it with your favorite dippers, and watch it disappear as everyone enjoys the delicious combination of creamy cheese and crispy bacon.

Irish Potato Bites

Ingredients:

- 1 1/2 pounds small red or gold potatoes, halved
- 2 tablespoons olive oil
- 1 teaspoon garlic powder
- 1 teaspoon dried thyme
- Salt and black pepper, to taste
- 1 cup shredded Irish cheddar cheese
- 1/4 cup chopped fresh chives
- Sour cream, for dipping

Instructions:

Preheat your oven to 400°F (200°C). Line a baking sheet with parchment paper.
In a large bowl, toss the halved potatoes with olive oil, garlic powder, dried thyme, salt, and black pepper until the potatoes are evenly coated.
Arrange the seasoned potato halves on the prepared baking sheet in a single layer.
Bake in the preheated oven for 20-25 minutes or until the potatoes are golden brown and tender, flipping them halfway through the cooking time.
Remove the potatoes from the oven and sprinkle the shredded Irish cheddar cheese over the top.
Return the baking sheet to the oven for an additional 3-5 minutes or until the cheese is melted and bubbly.
Remove from the oven and sprinkle the Irish Potato Bites with chopped fresh chives.
Serve the potato bites hot with a side of sour cream for dipping.
Enjoy these delicious and cheesy Irish Potato Bites as a tasty appetizer or snack!

These Irish Potato Bites are a delightful twist on traditional potato appetizers, featuring small red or gold potatoes topped with melted Irish cheddar cheese and fresh chives.

They are perfect for parties, game day, or as a savory snack. The combination of crispy potato skins, gooey cheese, and flavorful herbs makes them a crowd-pleaser. Serve them with sour cream for dipping and enjoy the delicious flavors of Ireland in bite-sized form!

Irish Stout Ice Cream

Ingredients:

- 2 cups heavy cream
- 1 cup whole milk
- 3/4 cup granulated sugar
- 4 large egg yolks
- 1 cup Irish stout beer (such as Guinness)
- 1 teaspoon vanilla extract
- Dark chocolate chunks or shavings (optional)

Instructions:

In a saucepan, heat the heavy cream and whole milk over medium heat until it just begins to simmer. Remove from heat.
In a mixing bowl, whisk together the sugar and egg yolks until well combined.
Slowly pour the hot cream and milk mixture into the egg and sugar mixture, whisking constantly to prevent curdling.
Pour the combined mixture back into the saucepan and cook over low heat, stirring constantly, until the mixture thickens and coats the back of a spoon. Do not let it boil.
Remove from heat and let the custard cool to room temperature.
Once cooled, stir in the Irish stout beer and vanilla extract.
Refrigerate the mixture for at least 4 hours or overnight.
Churn the chilled custard mixture in an ice cream maker according to the manufacturer's instructions.
If desired, add dark chocolate chunks or shavings during the last few minutes of churning.
Transfer the churned ice cream to a lidded container and freeze for an additional 4 hours or until firm.
Scoop and enjoy this rich and creamy Irish Stout Ice Cream with the distinctive flavor of Guinness!

This Irish Stout Ice Cream is a luscious and indulgent treat that combines the rich and malty flavor of Irish stout beer, such as Guinness, with a creamy custard base. The result is a velvety ice cream with a unique depth of taste. The addition of dark chocolate chunks or shavings enhances the experience with a hint of bitterness. It's a perfect dessert for St. Patrick's Day or any time you want to savor the distinctive flavors of Ireland in frozen form.

Irish Cheddar and Ale Soup

Ingredients:

- 4 tablespoons unsalted butter
- 1 large onion, finely chopped
- 2 carrots, peeled and diced
- 2 celery stalks, diced
- 3 cloves garlic, minced
- 1/2 cup all-purpose flour
- 4 cups chicken or vegetable broth
- 2 cups Irish ale (such as Guinness)
- 1 bay leaf
- 1 teaspoon dried thyme
- 1 teaspoon Worcestershire sauce
- 2 cups shredded sharp Irish cheddar cheese
- 1 cup half-and-half or heavy cream
- Salt and black pepper, to taste
- Chopped fresh chives, for garnish
- Croutons or crusty bread, for serving

Instructions:

In a large pot, melt the butter over medium heat.
Add the chopped onion, diced carrots, diced celery, and minced garlic to the pot. Cook until the vegetables are softened, about 5-7 minutes.
Sprinkle the flour over the vegetables and stir well to coat.
Gradually whisk in the chicken or vegetable broth, ensuring there are no lumps.
Pour in the Irish ale, add the bay leaf, dried thyme, and Worcestershire sauce. Stir to combine.
Bring the soup to a simmer and let it cook for 15-20 minutes, allowing the flavors to meld and the vegetables to become tender.
Remove the bay leaf and discard.
Reduce the heat to low, and gradually add the shredded Irish cheddar cheese, stirring until melted and smooth.
Stir in the half-and-half or heavy cream, and let the soup heat through without boiling.
Season the soup with salt and black pepper to taste. Adjust the seasoning if needed.

Ladle the Irish Cheddar and Ale Soup into bowls.
Garnish with chopped fresh chives and serve with croutons or crusty bread.
Enjoy this comforting and flavorful Irish Cheddar and Ale Soup!

This Irish Cheddar and Ale Soup is a rich and hearty dish that combines the bold flavors of Irish ale and sharp cheddar cheese. The result is a creamy and comforting soup with a depth of taste that is perfect for warming up on a chilly day. Serve it with croutons or crusty bread for a delightful meal that captures the essence of Irish cuisine.

Leprechaun Hat S'mores

Ingredients:

- Marshmallows
- Chocolate bars or chocolate chips
- Graham crackers
- Green candy melts or green chocolate
- Yellow candy or yellow icing

Instructions:

Preheat your oven to broil.
Break the graham crackers in half to form squares.
Place half of the graham crackers on a baking sheet and top each with a marshmallow.
Place the baking sheet under the broiler for 1-2 minutes or until the marshmallows are golden brown and puffed. Keep a close eye to prevent burning.
Remove the baking sheet from the oven and place a piece of chocolate on top of each marshmallow.
In a microwave-safe bowl, melt the green candy melts or green chocolate according to the package instructions.
Dip the top of each marshmallow and chocolate stack into the melted green candy to create the leprechaun hat.
Place the dipped s'mores on parchment paper to set.
Once the green candy coating has set, use yellow candy or yellow icing to create a buckle on each hat, resembling a leprechaun's hat.
Allow the Leprechaun Hat S'mores to cool and the candy coating to fully set.
Serve these festive treats as a delightful and whimsical addition to your St. Patrick's Day celebration!

These Leprechaun Hat S'mores are a playful and delicious way to celebrate St. Patrick's Day. With their cute leprechaun hat design, they are sure to bring smiles to both kids and adults. The combination of gooey marshmallows, melted chocolate, and the crunch of graham crackers makes them a delightful treat for the holiday festivities.

Irish Cheddar Soda Bread

Ingredients:

- 4 cups all-purpose flour
- 1 teaspoon baking soda
- 1 teaspoon salt
- 1 and 3/4 cups buttermilk
- 1 cup shredded Irish cheddar cheese
- 1/4 cup unsalted butter, melted

Instructions:

Preheat your oven to 425°F (220°C). Lightly grease a baking sheet or line it with parchment paper.
In a large mixing bowl, combine the all-purpose flour, baking soda, and salt.
Gradually add the buttermilk to the dry ingredients, mixing with a wooden spoon or your hands until a dough forms. The dough should be soft but not too sticky.
Fold in the shredded Irish cheddar cheese, ensuring it is evenly distributed throughout the dough.
Turn the dough out onto a floured surface and gently knead it a few times until it forms a round loaf.
Place the loaf on the prepared baking sheet. Use a sharp knife to score a deep "X" on the top of the loaf.
Brush the melted butter over the top of the loaf.
Bake in the preheated oven for 15 minutes. Then, reduce the oven temperature to 400°F (200°C) and continue baking for an additional 20-25 minutes or until the bread is golden brown and sounds hollow when tapped on the bottom.
Allow the Irish Cheddar Soda Bread to cool on a wire rack before slicing.
Serve the slices with additional butter if desired.
Enjoy this flavorful and cheesy Irish Cheddar Soda Bread as a delightful accompaniment to your St. Patrick's Day meal!

This Irish Cheddar Soda Bread is a savory and cheesy twist on the traditional Irish soda bread. The addition of shredded Irish cheddar cheese brings a rich and savory flavor to the bread, making it a perfect accompaniment to soups, stews, or as a delicious side for your St. Patrick's Day celebration. The crunchy crust and soft interior make it a delightful treat for any occasion.

Mint Chocolate Chip Cookies

Ingredients:

- 1 cup unsalted butter, softened
- 1 cup granulated sugar
- 1 cup packed brown sugar
- 2 large eggs
- 1 teaspoon vanilla extract
- 1 teaspoon peppermint extract
- 3 cups all-purpose flour
- 1 teaspoon baking soda
- 1/2 teaspoon baking powder
- 1/2 teaspoon salt
- 1 1/2 cups chocolate chips (semisweet or dark chocolate)
- 1/2 cup mint chocolate chips
- Green food coloring (optional)
- 1/2 cup chopped mint chocolate or Andes mint baking chips (optional)

Instructions:

Preheat your oven to 350°F (175°C). Line baking sheets with parchment paper.
In a large mixing bowl, cream together the softened butter, granulated sugar, and brown sugar until light and fluffy.
Add the eggs one at a time, beating well after each addition.
Stir in the vanilla extract and peppermint extract. If desired, add a few drops of green food coloring for a minty green color.
In a separate bowl, whisk together the flour, baking soda, baking powder, and salt.
Gradually add the dry ingredients to the wet ingredients, mixing until just combined.
Fold in the chocolate chips, mint chocolate chips, and chopped mint chocolate or Andes mint baking chips, if using.
Drop rounded tablespoons of dough onto the prepared baking sheets, spacing them about 2 inches apart.
Bake in the preheated oven for 10-12 minutes or until the edges are set and lightly golden.
Allow the cookies to cool on the baking sheets for a few minutes before transferring them to a wire rack to cool completely.

Enjoy these delightful Mint Chocolate Chip Cookies with a cool and refreshing mint flavor!

These Mint Chocolate Chip Cookies are a delicious and refreshing twist on the classic chocolate chip cookie. The combination of mint extract, chocolate chips, and optional mint chocolate pieces creates a delightful treat with a cool and minty flavor. Whether you're celebrating St. Patrick's Day or just craving a minty sweet indulgence, these cookies are sure to be a hit!

Irish Whiskey Chocolate Fondue

Ingredients:

- 8 ounces dark chocolate, finely chopped
- 1/2 cup heavy cream
- 2 tablespoons Irish whiskey
- 1/2 teaspoon vanilla extract
- Assorted dippables: strawberries, bananas, pineapple, marshmallows, pretzels, pound cake, etc.

Instructions:

In a heatproof bowl, place the finely chopped dark chocolate.
In a small saucepan, heat the heavy cream over medium heat until it just begins to simmer. Do not let it boil.
Pour the hot cream over the chopped chocolate and let it sit for a minute to soften the chocolate.
Gently stir the chocolate and cream mixture until smooth and well combined.
Stir in the Irish whiskey and vanilla extract until fully incorporated.
Transfer the chocolate fondue to a fondue pot or a heatproof bowl placed over a candle or fondue burner to keep it warm.
Arrange the assorted dippables on a serving platter.
Enjoy dipping the fruits, marshmallows, and other treats into the luscious Irish Whiskey Chocolate Fondue!

This Irish Whiskey Chocolate Fondue is a luxurious and indulgent treat that adds a touch of Irish flair to your dessert experience. The combination of rich dark chocolate, cream, and a hint of Irish whiskey creates a velvety fondue that's perfect for dipping a variety of delicious treats. It's a delightful way to celebrate St. Patrick's Day or any special occasion where you want to share a sweet and spirited treat with friends and family.